LOOKING AT PAINTINGS

Children

Three Studies of a Child Wearing a Cap, undated
Antoine Watteau, French (1684–1721)

LOOKING AT PAINTINGS

Children

Peggy Roalf

Series Editor
Jacques Lowe

Designer
Joseph Guglietti

Belitha Press
London

A
JACQUES LOWE
VISUAL ARTS PROJECTS
BOOK

Text © 1993 by Jacques Lowe Visual Arts Projects Inc.
A Jacques Lowe Visual Arts Projects Book

First published in the United States by Hyperion Books for Children.

First published in 1993 in the United Kingdom by

Belitha Press Ltd,
31 Newington Green, London N16 9PU.

Printed in Italy

Cataloguing in Print data available from the British Library

ISBN 1 85561 201 1

Original design concept by Amy Hill
UK Project editor: Jill Laidlaw
UK Editor: Kate Scarborough

Contents

To Kelly, to love, to children

Introduction

LOOKING AT PAINTINGS is a series of books about understanding what great artists see when they paint. Children have been a favourite subject for painters since the time of the ancient Egyptians. One of the earliest surviving portraits of a child was created seventeen hundred years ago by an unknown Egyptian artist (see page 9). He captured the bright eyes and proud expression of a boy named Eutyches in a painting that was wrapped with the boy's body when he was buried.

Pieter Brueghel (on page 15) created a scene that expresses every child's idea of fun. It was a world in which adults play no part. In *Children's Games*, a view from above of a village square completely taken over by young people, Brueghel illustrated more than eighty different games, many of which are still played today.

Artists working for kings and nobles have painted portraits that show what their wealthy **patrons'** ambitions were for their children. For example, Agnolo Bronzino portrayed Giovanni de' Medici (page 12) as an impish baby wearing luxurious silk clothes. Using expensive **pigments** and paint made from real gold, he painted a portrait that foretells Giovanni's future as a Roman Catholic cardinal.

When painters draw their own children, we can see expressions of love in images that mean a lot to the artists. The American artist Frank W. Benson captured the seemingly endless pleasure of his children's summer holiday in *Calm Morning*, a painting that glimmers with light reflected from a peaceful harbour (on page 34).

Great artists have expressed the joys and sorrows of young people from different times and places, often adding memories from their own childhood into the paintings. You can look at other children—your friends and classmates—and use your imagination to see them as a painter would.

Note: words in **bold** are explained in the glossary on pages 46 and 47.

PORTRAIT OF A BOY, second century A.D.
Unknown artist from Fayum, Egypt, encaustic on wood, 38 x 19 cm

This portrait of a boy named Eutyches was created by an Egyptian artist who lived during a period of Roman rule. Ancient Egyptian tomb paintings look like flat figures seen in profile with sharp outlines. When the Romans conquered Egypt, they copied the old fashion for mummifying bodies, but changed the style of painting. This portrait was wrapped around Eutyches' body. It shows the new way of painting that made the subject look more real.

Ancient painting techniques

The painter used great skill to achieve strong effects with only a few colours. Before man-made pigments came into use, painters used colours made from natural materials. Yellow, red and brown pigments were made from different types of clay. Black was made from charred bones or soot from oil lamps and white by roasting chalk or oyster shells in an oven.

The fresh colours in this portrait were made through a technique called encaustic, a word which comes from ancient Greek meaning 'to burn in'. The artist mixed the different pigments with beeswax melted over a hot fire and produced creamy **opaque** colours as well as thin **transparent** shades. When the painting was completed, the artist passed a hot metal pan over the surface to burn in the colours, permanently fixing them to the wooden panel on which he or she had painted.

The artist made the skin look lifelike by brushing transparent white over the evenly-painted face. The boy's eyes (see the close-up above) are highlighted with touches of white which gives them a realistic warmth. To create a rounded effect, the artist has added a few shadows to the right side of the head, nose and neck. Because all these features are still so clear, it is amazing to think that this painting is almost two thousand years old.

EDWARD VI AS A CHILD, about 1538
Hans Holbein the Younger, German (1497?–1543), oil on panel, 57 x 44.5 cm

Hans Holbein the Younger was taught by his father, a well-known painter in Augsburg, Germany. He became an established artist in Basel, Switzerland, while still a teenager. In 1536 Holbein became the official painter to Henry VIII of England.

Royal portraits

In this portrait of Edward, the son of Henry VIII and the third of his six wives, Jane Seymour, Holbein revealed royal power in a two-year-old boy. Grasping a golden rattle in one tiny hand, Edward raises the other in a kingly gesture and looks down out of the picture as though at his subjects below him. Because there are no everyday objects in the painting to compare in size with the figure, Edward seems larger than life.

*Ambrosius Holbein, Hans Holbein the Younger's brother, captured the thoughtful mood of this boy in a drawing. With a pointed silver rod, he made pale grey lines that turned black as the silver particles from the rod **tarnished.***

Costly paints

Using **oil paints** made of real gold and expensive red pigment, Holbein captured the softness of velvet and the stiffness of heavily embroidered silks. Using the technique of **foreshortening**, Holbein reduced the distance between the child's right hand and shoulder. This makes the appearance look in **proportion** when viewed straight on.

The Latin inscription adds to the formality of this portrait. It praises the little boy and the family and country into which he has been born and which he will one day rule.

Holbein's commanding portraits of England's royal family made him the favourite painter of Henry VIII. Holbein spent the rest of his life in England and practised a style of court portraiture that was popular for the next hundred years.

PARVVLE PATRISSA, PATRIÆ VIRTVTIS ET HÆRES
    ESTO, NIHIL MAIVS MAXIMVS ORBIS HABET.
GNATVM VIX POSSVNT COELVM ET NATVRA DEDISSE,
    HVIVS QVEM PATRIS, VICTVS HONORET HONOS.
ÆQVATO TANTVM, TANTI TV FACTA PARENTIS,
    VOTA HOMINVM, VIX QVO PROGREDIANTVR, HABENT
VINCITO, VICISTI, QVOT REGES PRISCVS ADORAT
    ORBIS, NEC TE QVI VINCERE POSSIT, ERIT.   Ricard. Morysing Car:~

GIOVANNI DE' MEDICI AT EIGHTEEN MONTHS, 1545
Agnolo Bronzino (born Agnolo di Cosimo), Italian (1503–72), tempera on panel, 58 x 48 cm

*a*gnolo Bronzino and his patron, Cosimo de' Medici, both gained influence and power through luck. When his distant relative Alessandro was murdered in 1537, Cosimo became duke of Florence. Soon after, he noticed Bronzino's talent when, as a young **apprentice**, Bronzino was working on a **mural** at the Medici palace. Cosimo chose Bronzino as his official painter.

Red for a cardinal

Bronzino added details to this portrait that hint at what Giovanni de' Medici's future was to be. Following tradition, as the second son of Cosimo, Giovanni would become a clergyman, whereas his older brother, Francesco, would inherit their father's title. Giovanni's wine-coloured tunic is the same colour as the red robes worn by cardinals of the Roman Catholic church. The goldfinch was a sign in paintings of the time for the infant Jesus Christ. So it is another link with the Church.

The child as an adult

Bronzino created a portrait that expresses the Medici family's position and ambition. The baby's amused and childlike expression does not seem to suit his adult clothes. His downy hair and chubby hands contrast with the upright pose and the stiff costume. These features make the baby seem more important. Bronzino created warm, lifelike skin tones by adding a transparent rosy **glaze** to the face and hands. The green background emphasizes the warm colours in the baby's face and clothing.

With a few smoothly drawn lines of chalk on coarse paper, Andrea del Verrocchio (1435–88) captured a sleepy infant's soft features.

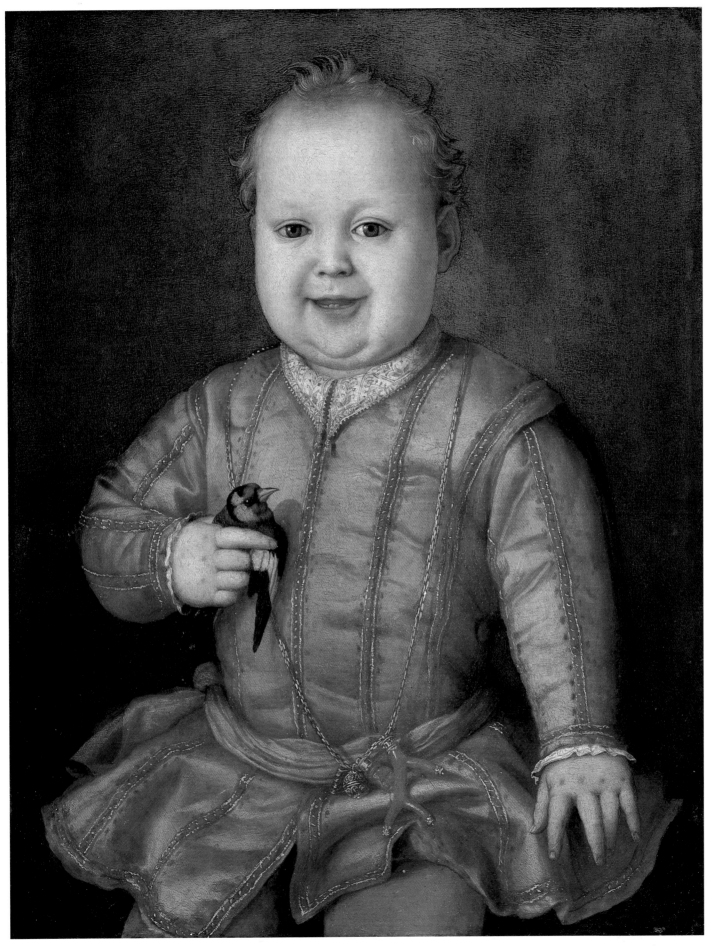

CHILDREN'S GAMES, 1560
Pieter Brueghel, Flemish (1525?–69), oil on oak panel, 123 x 161 cm

*P*ieter Brueghel often painted the joys and sorrows of Flemish country people. For sixteenth-century farmers, life consisted of back-breaking work, high taxes and constant war. Young people toiled as hard as their parents. When work came to a halt for religious holidays, they all made the most of their free time.

An overview

In this painting, Brueghel chose a high view looking down on a town square completely taken over by children. He created a visual encyclopedia of games: there are more than eighty different activities in this scene, from playing marbles and rolling hoops in the foreground, jousting on piggy-back in the middle to walking on stilts in the background.

Brueghel brought order to this busy scene by painting an impressive town building in the background. However, look at the children playing around it. Under the arches, they are spinning tops; they hang out of the windows and swing from its hitching gate. They are not treating it with the respect it seems to deserve. This is a typical feature in all of Brueghel's country paintings. He loved to paint country people's sense of humour and love of fun.

Through the careful balance of bright and soft colours, Brueghel made the figures stand out clearly from the golden earth. The red paint that he used for many of the costumes is dotted throughout the games and into the distant landscape where they continue. Although this painting is over 400 years old, how many games do you recognise?

Brueghel used light and dark colours to separate out the figures in this tug-of-war game.

14

BOY IN A CORAL NECKLACE, about 1619
Peter Paul Rubens, Flemish (1577–1640), black, white and red chalk on paper, 25 x 20 cm

Like many of the best painters of the time, Peter Paul Rubens had royal patrons, Archduke Albert and Archduchess Isabella, rulers of the Low Countries (present-day Belgium, Luxembourg and the Netherlands). They **commissioned** grand portraits to impress visiting foreign nobles. There was such a demand for Rubens' paintings that he trained assistants to help prepare the work. He made drawings, which the helpers **transferred** onto canvas. Following their master's precise instructions, the assistants applied the first layers of paint. Later, Rubens skilfully added the finer details and transparent coloured glazes. His mastery brought the paintings to life.

His own work

Away from the busy workshop and his demanding patrons, Rubens often made drawings, such as this one of his son, Nicolas. Using crayons harder than charcoal but softer than wax, Rubens captured the softness of Nicolas's face, his clear eyes and the feathery wisps of his hair. Rubens formed shadows with both grey and red fine, overlapping lines. This technique is called **cross-hatching.** He created highlights by carefully leaving areas blank on the necklace and the boy's lips, nose and eyelids. White chalk is used as a highlight only under the boy's chin and in his hair.

This picture, created by his hand alone, shows the real talent of the painter. It is not surprising that he was able to give the final touches to paintings to make them sparkle.

By using cross-hatching and leaving areas of paper blank , Rubens created an impression of light in this drawing of another son, Peter Paul. The artist made this study in preparation for the painting, Rubens, His Wife Hélèna Fourment, and Their Son Peter Paul.

P P Rubens

17

GEORGE AND FRANCIS VILLIERS, 1635
Anthony van Dyck, Flemish (1599–1641), oil on canvas, 137 x 127.5 cm

*A*nthony van Dyck, the most famous pupil of Peter Paul Rubens, moved from Belgium to England in 1632. As official painter to Charles I, Van Dyck painted portraits of the royal household, which included George and Francis Villiers. The two boys were brought up with Charles I's children after the death of their father, who had been the one of the king's closest friends and an important politician.

Using coloured chalk, Raphael (1483–1520) drew parallel curved lines that follow the shape of this boy's face to create shadows that make this drawing look realistic.

When you look at this painting there are two things which stand out: the boys' highly elaborate clothes, even down to the high-heeled shoes, and their confident, if not arrogant, expressions. They are obviously from a wealthy and influential family and Van Dyck painted this picture to show just that. There is also nothing in the portrait to show that these boys are children.

'Fat over lean'

Van Dyck uses an extraordinary painting technique to capture the shimmer, the movement—almost the rustling sound—of the boys' silk robes. This technique is called 'fat over lean'. Van Dyck would begin painting with dark colours thinned with a liquid called **turpentine**. After the thin, or lean, layer was dry, he applied brighter **tones**. These he thickened, or fattened, with oil, mixing the colours on the canvas while the paint was wet. Through this technique, Van Dyck ensured that the thicker layers of colour would not crack as the paint dried. Today the silk glows with the same clarity and brilliance that it originally had over 350 years ago.

Van Dyck concentrated on the main features of this portrait. Look carefully and you will see that the left hand of George (the boy on the left) is very rough compared to his right hand. What else can you see that looks unfinished?

19

PORTRAIT OF THE INFANTA MARGARITA, undated
Diego Rodríguez de Silva Velázquez, Spanish (1599–1660), oil on
canvas, 69.8 x 58 cm

King Philip IV of Spain struggled to keep his country from collapsing under the pressure of war with France. In an attempt to end the conflict between the two nations and form a more friendly alliance, Philip arranged the marriage of his daughter, Marie-Thérèse, to Louis XIV of France. As the two had never met and travel was dangerous and difficult, Philip commissioned portraits painted by the official court artist Diego Velázquez to send to the French court. Velázquez made the portraits as flattering as possible.

Margarita

Velázquez also painted a series of portraits of Margarita, the youngest and prettiest Spanish princess, to encourage her engagement to Leopold I of Austria. Every few years, Philip sent a new painting of Margarita to Leopold's parents as a sign of his friendship and, of course, to show off his beautiful daughter.

Layers of colour

Only a small number of colours were available to seventeenth-century European painters. However, in Velázquez's hands, the paint seems to bring his subjects to life. Velázquez first painted Margarita's gown in a bluish grey tone. Over this he applied a thin layer of white that allows the blue-grey tone to show through, creating the effect of folds in the fabric. The dark shadows, a typical feature of Velázquez's work, make the few colours—red, black, and white—shine out. Rather than trying to paint lifelike details, Velázquez was able to capture the light flickering across Margarita's satin rosettes and jewellery with dashes of thick white paint. Using the same bold brushwork, Velázquez painted Margarita's hair in a blur of colour that comes into focus with a few highlights.

DON MANUEL OSORIO MANRIQUE DE ZUÑIGA, about 1787–88
Francisco de Goya, Spanish (1746–1828), oil on canvas, 127 x 101.5 cm

Francisco de Goya was born in the poor, isolated village of Fuendetodos in Spain. Goya learned his craft as an apprentice artist in the city of Zaragoza. He moved to Madrid in 1763 where he struggled to make ends meet by working as an assistant. Whilst teaching at the Royal Academy, Goya made contact with noble families who commissioned portraits and murals. After several rejections, Goya was finally accepted as a painter to King Charles III of Spain in 1789.

Goya's style

In this portrait of the Count of Altamira's son, we see Goya's masterly skill in painting contrasting colours, textures and light. Goya painted Manuel's red suit in broad strokes with hardly any shadow or detail. In contrast, the white lace collar and satin sash glow with light, an effect made possible by delicately painted highlights. Goya emphasized the boy's rosy skin by contrasting it with a grey-green background.

What does the picture mean?

Goya displays his gift for telling a secret story in this picture. Standing alone in an empty room, the boy is surrounded by pets that represent both good and evil. The three menacing cats are poised to pounce on the magpie, a Christian symbol of goodness. The caged birds are supposed to represent childhood in the way that children are told what to do by adults.

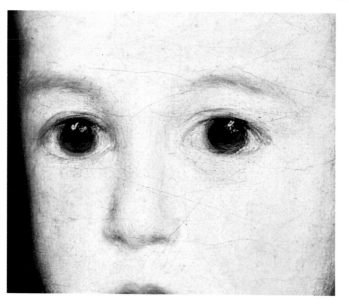

A detail of Manuel de Zúñiga's face shows that Goya defined the child's features with pink and the same grey-green colour of the background as in his portrait of Don Manuel..

ELS.^{Dⁿ} MANVEL OSORIO MANRRIQVE D ZVÑIGA

BABY IN RED HIGH CHAIR, about 1800–25
Unknown American artist, oil on canvas, 55.8 x 38.7 cm

*A*merican **folk art** grew as a tradition far removed from wealthy drawing rooms in the American state of New England and great farms in the South. Artists who had studied in Europe created graceful portraits and landscape paintings that were fashionable amongst their rich clients. Largely unknown artists mostly living in the country painted for different people. These painters probably earned their living **sign painting** and decorating but had had no traditional training. Through observation and imagination they created simple, but often expressive, paintings to record important events in the lives of ordinary people.

An artist from Pennsylvania captured the angelic expression of this sleeping infant. With delicate touches of reddy-brown paint, the artist defined the baby's features and downy hair. The painter emphasized the softness of the baby, its clothing and its blanket through the contrast between ivory and peach and the black background.

Unschooled

You can tell that this artist had no formal training, because the child does not look lifelike. The pose seems unnatural, even uncomfortable, and there is no sense of depth either to the baby or the chair. However, the painting's charm comes from the baby's chubby body, rosy cheeks and smile. The figure, large in proportion to the size of the canvas, engages us with its simplicity and clear expression.

Although this country painting was done almost two hundred years ago, it could have been done today, because its style seems so modern.

In 1837, American folk artist Isaac Sheffield (dates unknown) painted this portrait of James Francis Smith to celebrate his return from a whaling expedition to the Antarctic. In the background, Sheffield included the ship on which Smith had travelled.

THE FIFE PLAYER 1866
Edouard Manet, French (1832–83), oil on canvas, 160 x 96.5 cm

Today it is difficult to know why Edouard Manet's paintings shocked the people of his time. Even this portrait of a young fife player provoked harsh comments. One critic wrote that it looked flat, like a playing card illustration. Art experts of the nineteenth century preferred paintings that made human activity glorious through the choice of historical themes or through carefully painted art. Manet, however, often depicted ordinary people, such as this young cadet. He simplified details to create a strong impact, but for many of the people around him this effect gave the impression of an unfinished work.

Manet's new style

One of the differences between Manet and the artists who followed the old style of painting was the use of shadows. Formal schools trained artists to look at figures as a series of shadows and in this way the artist would be able to give their subjects depth. Manet felt that this was artificial. If you look at a person in daylight, there is often very little difference between the shaded areas and unshaded. If you look with your eyes as opposed to thinking about what should be right you will see that this is true.

The example

This picture is a perfect example of what Manet was trying to achieve. He drew the fifer straight on, leaving the largest area for the costume, which he painted in blocks of strong colours: red, black and white. Areas of scarlet paint form the trousers. Two curving bands of black outline the figure and give it shape. Look at the jacket. You can hardly see the outline of the boy's left arm, but you know that it's there. By giving the figure no definition, Manet was deliberately going against tradition.

THE DAUGHTERS OF EDWARD D. BOIT, 1882
John Singer Sargent, American (1856–1925), oil on canvas, 221 x 221 cm

John Singer Sargent's parents believed that the cultural centres of Europe would provide the best education for their children. Sargent's father gave up a medical practice in Philadelphia and moved the family to Florence, Italy, where the artist was born in 1856. After completing his studies in Paris, Sargent painted this group portrait of the daughters of his friend Edward Boit, an American artist who also lived in the French capital.

Art as photography
Sargent was fascinated by photography, which had recently become popular because of small hand-held cameras. In a painting that is more than two metres high, Sargent imitated the qualities of a snapshot. Even the square shape, unusual for a painting, is the same as many photographs of the time. His young subjects look with questioning eyes at the viewer, as though interrupted during an important activity. Sargent painted the two figures in the foreground as well as the magnificent carpet in sharp focus. He blurred the distant figures like the out-of-focus background often seen in photographs.

The pose
Sargent painted a room filled with objects that are enormous compared to the children. He posed the four girls in a vast, empty hall whose dark walls disappear into dark shadows. Their white pinafores stand out clearly in the spacious foreground as does the glowing window at the back of the room. The girls all look small because the artist has put them near large objects, like the carpet and the vases. Compare this to the Van Dyck picture on page 19 where the two Villiers boys look fully grown and therefore seemingly more important.

In this detail, we can see that Sargent painted broad strokes of white on the girl's dress that look realistic when seen from a distance.

CHILDREN PLAYING ON THE BEACH, 1884
Mary Cassatt, American (1844–1926), oil on canvas, 97.7 x 74 cm

Mary Cassatt decided to become a artist during a family visit to Europe when she was seven years old. She was inspired by the great paintings she saw in art museums and galleries there. After completing four years of training back in the United States at the Pennsylvania Academy of Fine Arts, Cassatt moved to Paris, France. Only three years later, Cassatt successfully exhibited her work at the 1868 **Paris Salon.**

A simple picture?

Although this picture looks like a simple snapshot, Cassatt spent time carefully organizing the **composition** by making detailed drawings. Repeated angles, shapes, and colours focus our attention on two toddlers absorbed in play. Their arms and legs and a toy spade—positioned at angles—slant into the picture.

An Impressionist style

Cassatt was deeply influenced by the new French **Impressionists** (Edouard Manet on page 26 was one of the earliest of these painters). In this picture, Cassatt captured an impression of the bright but shadowless quality of sunlight on a hazy sky. With strong colours, she painted the children's sunburned faces and arms. Highlights of thick white paint sparkle like reflected light on the pinafores. The toned down greys and blues in the distant ocean and sky make the figures seem

Edgar Degas made this drawing of Giovanna Bellelli in preparation for a large group portrait of her family. He drew the shadows by crosshatching, using black chalk on pink paper.

brighter by contrast. In 1873, Mary Cassatt's talent came to the attention of the great French artist Edgar Degas (1834–1917), also an Impressionist. Degas became a longtime friend and mentor to the gifted American painter.

Mary Cassatt

TO CELEBRATE THE BABY (Child with Puppet), 1903
Henri Rousseau, French (1844–1910), oil on canvas, 100.25 x 81 cm

Henri Rousseau worked as an inspector for the customs department in Paris and could only paint on Sundays. When he retired in 1893 to become a full-time artist, Rousseau endured extreme poverty in order to paint. Being a painter was the life Rousseau had dreamed of, and his sense of wonder and joy comes through in his work.

Like American folk artists (see pages 24 and 25), Rousseau was self-taught. But unlike those mostly country artists, Rousseau studied paintings in the Louvre museum and in the art galleries of Paris. Through hard work and constant study, Rousseau created a new painting style.

Painting every detail

Rousseau exaggerated the size of the child compared to the landscape to give the child more importance. The baby's pale complexion, white gown and chubby form are very different from the brightly painted puppet constructed of hard-edged shapes and sharp angles. Rousseau's great achievement in his paintings was to depict every detail. Every leaf on every tree and each blade of grass is individually painted, even the wispy hair of the child. Rousseau proved that you do not have to be trained to produce lively and bright pictures. He just used simple colours and clear outlines to create a strong image.

In this amusing family portrait, Rousseau depicts a baby that appears to be older and wiser than the adults.

Rousseau's paintings were admired in his lifetime by the public and by other more well-known artists, including **Pablo Picasso** (1881–1973). But Rousseau was a poor businessman. He often sold his work for the price of a cheap meal and gave music lessons to make ends meet. When he died, he was buried in a pauper's grave.

CALM MORNING, 1904
Frank W. Benson, American (1862–1951), oil on canvas, 111.7 x 91.4 cm

*E*very summer Frank W. Benson moved with his family to an island farmhouse off the coast of Maine in North America. Benson enjoyed the unspoiled natural beauty of the North Atlantic coast and created many portraits of his children in these perfect surroundings.

In *Calm Morning*, Benson captured the bliss of a holiday in a place where the sun always shines. In this painting, Benson posed three of his children—George, Elisabeth and Sylvia—in a triangle that is the centre of the picture. Because he painted this from the bank above the children, you get a better view of inside the boat. Through the use of **perspective**, he created an effect of depth and space by painting sailing boats getting smaller and smaller as they sail nearer the horizon.

Coloured highlights

Benson painted hazy sunlight with golden highlights and shadows with a pale blue colour. He captured the light inside the boat with curving strokes of yellow and blue paint that also show the shape of the hull. Using the same colours, he added soft shadows to the children's white clothes. A few swirls of paint in deeper shades of yellow and blue capture the light reflecting up from the water onto the bottom of the boat.

This picture demonstrates how Benson was fascinated by the changing light and colours of the flat sea on the coast of Maine. He used soft lighting and colour tones to capture the peaceful beauty of a calm harbour.

For this portrait of Alice Trask, Thomas Anschutz (1851–1912) used pastels—soft sticks of coloured chalk—to depict the variety of textures in her fur coat, silk ribbon and wool hat.

PORTRAIT OF CLAUDE RENOIR, CALLED COCO, about 1906
Pierre-Auguste Renoir (1841–1919), oil on canvas laid on board, 16.5 x 12.7 cm

Pierre-Auguste Renoir painted lively pictures of graceful landscapes, busy race-courses, happy children and beautiful women. This portrait of his youngest son, Claude, nicknamed Coco, declares the fatherly love and pride Renoir felt for the child who was born when the painter was fifty-nine years old. He captured Coco's youth in a portrait that seems to radiate with light and energy.

In this full-length portrait of Robert Nunès, Renoir emphasized line through the angular pose, the boy's clearly outlined features, and the striped trimming on the suit.

Painting progress

In the 1880s, Renoir experienced a crisis in his work. He believed that he was not progressing as a painter. In his search for a new style, he developed an oil painting technique very much like **water-colour** methods. In this portrait, which is a quickly-made study for a large painting, we can see how Renoir worked. First, he sketched the picture directly onto the canvas, using a brush and red-brown paint **diluted** with turpentine. When this layer was dry, he added highlights on Coco's face and hair with light colours, again thinned with turpentine. The first layer of red-brown paint, which also covers the background, glows through the highlights to give a soft, realistic effect we can almost touch and feel. Clean lavender-coloured shadows go well with the golden highlights on Coco's hair, face and shirt. Because Renoir mixed colours directly on the canvas like a watercolourist, rather than on his **palette**, he kept the pure freshness of the colours.

Although this painting looks as though it was done quickly, it was not without effort and skill. Even when he was much older and suffering from arthritis, Renoir continued to adapt his technique, even though he was working with brushes taped to his crippled hands.

37

GIRL WITH BRAIDS, 1918
Amedeo Modigliani, Italian (1884–1920), oil on canvas, 54.5 x 45.6 cm

Like other young painters from all over the world, Amedeo Modigliani was attracted to the Paris art world. Fascinated by the art he had seen in a natural history museum, Modigliani put aside painting and began to carve sculpture. He created long, thin heads in simple forms that suggest Stone Age carvings. Because of poor health, which worsened due to alcohol and drugs, Modigliani could not keep up the physical effort needed to sculpt. He returned to painting and drew haunting portraits that were similar to the style of his sculpture.

A sculpted painting

In this painting, Modigliani simplified the young girl's figure, avoiding distracting details in the way a sculptor chips away at a block of stone. As in his sculpture, Modigliani emphasized shapes, like the oval head and eyes, the triangular nose and the rectangular forms in the background. The shape of the canvas makes the girl seem longer and thinner.

Modigliani added to the simple lines and shapes by using bold colours of red, green, black and white. Warm red tones—in the face, the shirt and the background—make us notice the girl's green eyes even more. To give a sense of depth, Modigliani applied a bright area of white behind the figure.

Two years after he created this portrait, Modigliani received his first public acclaim through an exhibition held in London. He died the following year, his life cut short by a drug overdose.

Pierre Bonnard (1867–1947) illustrated the awkward movement of a little girl burdened by a heavy basket by painting her struggling figure as a silhouette.

39

NELLIE WITH TOY, 1925
Otto Dix, German (1891–1969), oil and tempera on wood, 54 x 39.3 cm

Otto Dix was inspired by fifteenth-century **Renaissance** art. In *Nellie with Toy*, we can see that Dix was very influenced by the Holbein portrait which appears on page 11.

Dix portrays his daughter as a princess and shows us the emotions of a young child struggling to assert her will. In place of a tiara, she wears an outrageous pink bow. Before her are the symbols of royal power: a tower of wooden rings is her sceptre; a shocking pink ball, her orb. She confronts the viewer, tearfully defying any challenge to her authority.

Painting in tempera

Dix created the brilliant colours and **enamel**-like finish in **tempera**, a painstaking technique originally perfected during the Renaissance. In tempera, every aspect of the composition must first be studied in a drawing called a **cartoon**, which becomes the painter's working plan. Pure pigments are blended in advance; each colour is then combined with an equal amount of fresh egg yolk, which makes the pigment into a thick liquid.

After transferring the cartoon onto the panel, Dix mixed the tempera with water to allow the paint to flow from the brush. He first shaped the large areas—Nellie's face, her clothes, the background—in thinly painted transparent layers. He 'hatched' in shading, highlights and details with distinct brushstrokes that allow the colours beneath to glow through.

41

L'IL SIS, 1944
William H. Johnson, American (1901–70), oil on canvas, 66 x 54 cm

William H. Johnson was an African-American painter who received his formal training at the New York Academy of Design. Early in his career, he worked in a style inspired by great painters such as **Vincent van Gogh** (1853–90). After a 1932 visit to Africa, where he explored his origins, Johnson developed what he called a 'primitive' style of painting to express his feelings about the black experience. He then turned to memories of his own childhood in the rural South.

Johnson painted the doll's pram wheels to make them look fragile and unstable yet full of movement.

'Primitive' art

In this portrait of his niece, Johnson used only six colours: red, yellow, blue, green, brown and white. He painted the figure and doll carriage in expressive and simple forms set against an empty background. He painted a few details—the girl's fingernails and toenails and her hair ribbon—in a bold and clear style.

Use of colour

Through the use of colours that appear to advance or recede, Johnson created the sensation of depth and space. Using pairs of complementary colours, he created strong contrasts. Johnson mixed clear, bright shades of blue, green, and red that seem closer to us than the yellow background. Through the dark skin tone, Johnson depicted the girl in a space defined by colour rather than by traditional perspective drawing.

GIRL ON A BALCONY, 1983
Fernando Botero, Colombian (born 1932), oil on canvas, 122 x 88.8 cm

Fernando Botero decided to become an artist when he was a teenager in Colombia. At twenty-one, Botero moved to Italy to continue his education. There he studied the murals of **Andrea Mantegna** (1431–1506). In the fifteenth century, Mantegna was one of the painters who was most skilled in drawing objects in perspective.

Larger-than-life
Inspired by the grand proportions of Andrea Mantegna's larger-than-life figures, Botero began to exaggerate the size of the people he painted. By drawing figures that are extremely fat, Botero tells us about his point of view that large is beautiful.

Botero depicts this young girl as a majestic figure with billowing coils of hair. The buttons of her dress, the cherry earrings and the landscape of balloon-like trees emphasize her roundness.

Layers of paint
Botero built up the girl's ample form in thin layers of paint on a canvas covered with a salmon pink base layer of paint. The original layer of pink paint glows through the pale skin tones. He painted facial features and hands that are tiny compared to the figure. He used cool colours and applied them with even brushstrokes to create a smooth finish that is like china.

Contemporary artist Jim Dine (born 1935) made a drawing that looks like a painting through the use of charcoal, which he softened and blended with a brush dipped in oil.

Although this figure is greatly distorted, Botero avoids making fun of his subject through his gentle sense of humour and polished technical skill.

Glossary and Index

ANDREA MANTEGNA (1430/1-1506): an Italian painter who adopted a strong style early in his career. This style was extremely strong on **perspective**. Mantegna saw everything in three dimensions, as proved by the fact that he designed his own home in Mantua.

APPRENTICE: some one who works for a professional artist as a general helper. In this way the assistant learns the trade.

CARTOON: a full-size, detailed drawing on heavy paper that the artist **transfers** onto the painting surface as a guide. The term is derived from the Italian name of the paper, *cartone*.

COMMISSION: a work of art that a **patron** has asked the painter to produce.

COMPOSITION: the way the subjects in a picture are put together or composed.

CROSS-HATCHING: a drawing technique for shading, using fine, criss-crossed parallel lines.

DILUTED: the thinning of a liquid by adding another liquid like water or **turpentine.**

ENAMEL: (1) a **glaze** made of powdered coloured glass, applied to metal and baked, or fired, at a high temperature to produce a shiny surface. (2) paint that has a shiny, smooth surface when it dries.

FOLK ART: a term to describe objects or paintings that are made in a traditional way by craftsmen or painters who have had no formal art school training.

FORESHORTENING: *see also* PERSPECTIVE

GLAZE: a layer of a partly **transparent** colour that gives a glassy finish to the painting.

IMPRESSIONISTS: a group of mainly French painters in the late 19th century who painted exactly what they saw and did not follow traditional teachings about colour and light.

MURAL: a very large painting that decorates a wall or is created as part of a wall. Also called a wall painting.

OIL PAINT: **pigment** is combined with oil (usually linseed or poppy oil). Oil paint is never mixed with water. It is washed off brushes with **turpentine.** Oil paint dries slowly, which enables the artist to work on a painting for a long time. Oil paint has been used since the fifteenth century.

OPAQUE: not letting light pass through. Opaque paints conceal what is under them. (The opposite of **transparent**)

PABLO PICASSO (1881-1973): the most famous artist of this century and one of the most influential. He was born in Spain, but moved to Paris in 1904. He was not only a painter, he was also a sculptor, a potter and a designer.

PALETTE: (1) a flat tray used by a painter for laying out and mixing colours. (2) the range of colours selected by a painter for a work.

PARIS SALON: this was an annual exhibition held to show off the most fashionable artists of the year.

PATRON: one who supports the arts or an individual artist.

PERSPECTIVE: perspective is a method of representing people, places and things in a painting or drawing to make them appear solid or realistic rather than flat.

In addition, a special technique of perspective, called **foreshortening,** is used to make figures and objects painted on a flat surface look real. For example, an artist will paint the hand of an outstretched arm larger than it is in proportion to the arm, which becomes smaller as it goes back towards the shoulder. This correction, necessary in a picture using perspective, is automatically made by the human eye observing a scene in real life. **Foreshortening** refers to the representation of figures or objects, whereas **perspective** refers to the representation of a scene or a space.

PIGMENT: the raw material that that gives paint its colour. It can be made from natural or man-made minerals.

PROPORTION: the relation of one thing to another in size.

RENAISSANCE: a period of European history from the early 14th to late 16th century. The name means 'rebirth' in French and marks the change from the Middle Ages to the Modern Age. The rebirth refers to the revival of arts, literature, politics, trade, sciences and medicine.

SIGN PAINTING: the art of painting signs for shops.

TARNISHED: when a metal like silver comes into contact with the air it changes its colour slightly. This change of colour is called tarnished. It is similar to the rusting of iron.

TEMPERA: **pigment** is combined with a water-based substance. The paint is combined with raw egg yolk to turn it into a thick paste that can be applied with a brush. Tempera was used by the ancient Greeks and was the favourite method of painters in medieval Europe.

TONE: the colours used overall in a painting. For example, an artist might begin by painting the entire picture in shades of greenish grey. After more colours are applied using **transparent glazes,** shadows, and highlights, the mass of greenish grey colour underneath will show through as an even tone.

TRANSFERRED: this normally means moved from one place to another. However, in this sense, a cartoon that is moved is done by placing the original drawing over the canvas. The assistant then goes over the lines of the drawing with a series of pin-pricks. Charcoal is then rubbed over the drawing and it goes through the pin-pricks onto the canvas underneath. The canvas now has an accurate copy of the original cartoon transferred onto it.

TRANSPARENT: allowing light to pass through so colours underneath can be seen. (The opposite of **opaque**.)

TURPENTINE: a strong-smelling liquid made from pine sap, used in oil painting. *See also* OIL PAINT

VINCENT VAN GOGH (1853-90): a Dutch painter whose vigorous style became extremely popular, sadly after his death. He used colour as a way of expressing different moods rather then trying to paint exactly what he saw.

WATER-COLOUR: **pigment** is combined with a water-based subtance. Water-colour paint is thinned with water, and areas of paper are often left uncovered to produce highlights. Water-colour paint was first used 37,000 years ago by cave dwellers who created the first wall paintings.

Credits